MW01241935

Through the Eyes of Insignificance

Through the Eyes of Insignificance

Lessons from The Insignificant Man

Michael A. Rogers

Copyright © 2019 Michael A. Rogers
All Rights Reserved
ISBN-9781075716935

Dedication

This book is lovingly dedicated to Jesus, the Lord of my life.
To Debra, the love of my life.
To Daaron, my son of whom I couldn't be more proud.
To all those who have walked with us through the fiercest of storms:
Dr. Ball, Fred Adams, Gary Mason, Wendy and Rob Wight, and all those
who have lifted us daily in prayer.
To all who have helped us in any way.

May God richly bless each and every one of you!!

Table of Contents

Preface

Through the Eyes of Insignificance is the story of my immediate family. However, it is not the whole story. It is simply my perspective on a period of about eight years. My perspective is shaped by life events, some of which came long before this portion of our story began. In my life I have been a Youth Pastor, a music teacher at a public school, an administrative assistant at a charter school, and a private counselor. I have worked as a driver of flat beds for a hardware company and a barista for a coffee house. Currently I am an Elementary School Counselor. Course work in pastoral ministry and music theory and composition and a masters degree in counseling round out my education. These varied educational opportunities, as well as my life events, shape my perspective on our story.

The story is also constantly changing and growing. My views are not concrete, especially when it comes to my view of God. My beliefs regarding His actions, His love and power, His healing touch have continued to grow and change. I think this is important, as relationships are not static, but living, growing, and changing.

In a living, growing relationship, stagnation and concrete thinking are the enemy. When we hear phrases which tend to place God in a box and elevate our thinking to the place of the final word on God, we can be sure of only one thing: we are absolutely clueless. God is so far beyond our thoughts, His thinking so far beyond our thinking, His ways so far beyond our ways that to say we grasp a true understanding of God is absolute arrogance.

And yet, this God, this unimaginably loving, powerful creator wants to speak to us, desires to be found and heard by us. We read this in the one book which provides the words of God, words that are completely testable and verifiable. In His word we get a glimpse of what God is like, what His many attributes are, and we can have something with which to verify or falsify our own experiences and thoughts. This word, the living word of God, is what I use to test the events and thoughts which are shared in the following pages. I encourage you to do the same.

Read the story of my family's suffering and triumph. Enter into our trials and victories. Taste the despair, and follow it up with a drink of hope. Listen to the dismissive voices, but hear the heart of God. Feel the pain of my wife and son, and then feel the warm arms of our loving creator. Smell the stale scent of apathy and unbelief, and inhale the sweet scent of victory found in Jesus. Look at the world through our eyes, the eyes of insignificant people looking for help, crying in pain, and being shown how truly insignificant we are in a world full of apathy. And then, turn your gaze to the loving eyes of the Almighty Creator, and find in them true significance.

Through the Eyes of Insignificance is my story of finding significance in the arms of the Almighty Creator, the King of kings, the Lord of lords. It has many lessons learned, and hopefully shared, in a way which burrows into the brain and ends in the heart and soul. It is my prayer that this story will lift the veil of apathy, drive people to find significance in Jesus, and pour down revival on the land. May God bless you!

Michael A. Rogers
The Insignificant Man
Saturday, May 25, 2019

Chapter One

The End of Our World

For it is a dreadful truth that the state of (as you say) "having to depend solely on God" is what we all dread most. And of course that just shows how very much, how almost exclusively, we have been depending on things. But trouble goes so far back in our lives and is now so deeply ingrained, we will not turn to him as long as He leaves us anything else to turn to. I suppose all one can say is that it was bound to come. In the hour of death and the day of judgement, what else shall we have? Perhaps when those moments come, they will feel happiest who have been forced (however unwittingly) to begin practicing it here on earth. It is good of Him to force us; but dear me, how hard to feel that it is good at the time.

- C. S. Lewis Letters to an American Lady (16 December 1925)

"Mom's having bad chest pains Dad! She can hardly breathe!" and in a panicked voice, "She's convulsing!" Daaron's voice shouted through the phone.

Knowing he was home alone with his mother, my wife Debra, I told him to hang up the phone and assured him, "I'm on my way!" It was the hardest thing I'd had to tell my thirteen-year-old son. I dialed 9-1-1 while driving home as fast as I dared. My heart was racing and I was fighting back tears as I pulled in front of our house just as the ambulance arrived. Quickly the EMT loaded Debra for transport and Daaron and I followed in the car.

As we rounded a bend in the road, tears began to fill my sight. Daaron and I both cried, thinking this was the end of our world, that I was losing my wife of 17 years. I looked at Daaron and had a quick, quiet, tear-filled conversation with him as we both acknowledged what we thought to be coming. This would be the end; our lives would change. It was January 2013 and everything would be different from here on out. And so it was, though not in the way we thought.

We calmed ourselves and walked into the Emergency Room. I prepared myself for the worst, or at least the worst I could conceive of. Debra was convulsing on the examination table, crying out in abdominal pain. The ER staff ran their tests; scanned results, then came in and reported their stunning conclusion. "There is nothing wrong with your wife."

I sat there stunned, angry, silenced by the paradox of what I saw and what I'd heard the hospital staff say. My wife was 95 pounds, according to the hospital scales, meaning she had lost over 50 pounds in approximately two years' time. Her skin was colorless. Her eyes were lifeless. Her body shook as if she were being electrocuted. She was screaming in pain. Debra complained of a metal taste in her mouth and the feeling of being poisoned.

13

Yet the only solution offered by the physician was, "Does she have a psychiatrist?" I was livid; I wanted to launch myself at the doctor's throat.

I was angry! Furious because I know my wife! I am a counselor. I know psychosomatic illness and what Debra had was not psychosomatic. The fact that I'd carried my wife to the bathroom every fifteen minutes throughout the nights previous to this crisis told me this wasn't simply an illness in her mind. The fact that her body had radically deteriorated, going from healthy, whole, and strong, to completely bedridden over a period of two years, losing its color, its weight, its abilities, told me this wasn't mental illness. Yet the staff at the hospital obviously disagreed.

Just as they were going to release her, she went into more convulsions on the table. They placed her in the hospital for more tests, but the looks on the doctors' and nurses' faces revealed their diagnosis: They thought it was all psychological. I found out later no one would help her to the bathroom when she called for assistance. Instead, they let her wet her bed and lie in it. One nurse, who was there to help her get to the bathroom, said, "Well, I'm not going to carry you!" and gave her a shove in the back, causing my wife to stumble and almost collapse. Staff rolled their eyes at the "crazy" woman at the end of the hall. On one occasion I walked up behind a nurse as she ridiculed Debra, mimicking her unstable walk for the entertainment of other nurses. Seeing me approach from behind the woman, her audience got very quiet. She turned, stammered and stuttered, trying to white wash what she was doing. I furiously let her know what I thought of her, then simply walked away in anger. By the time they discharged Debra with a prescription for Xanax we were completely demoralized. It had been, by far, the worst hospital experience of our lives.

We took Debra home with no answers, no help, no change. Loneliness and despair threatened to overwhelm me as, once again, we were on our own; with one exception, one all-powerful person in our favor, my friend, my king, my Lord, Jesus Christ. We prayed fervently and then simply listened. My wife, shaking, crying in pain, listened; I listened; our son listened. God spoke. God did not let us down. He spoke simply. He spoke in a way my wife, in her sick state, could understand. Debra spoke quietly to me, "This is what I'm hearing, Mike."

Listening prayer, in itself, was not new to us. Over the last few months she had confided in me that God had told her she had a disease, but it was treatable. However, this time she told me there were more things she saw and heard as we prayed; the number 1, followed by the word "copper"; then she saw a list of numbers, followed by blanks, as if there was a list of things which God was going to reveal as we followed each step. This list was consistently brought to mind and pushed us on, although we did not know precisely what it all meant. But, it was all we had and we clung tenaciously to His voice.

Almost seven years later, we still cling to His voice. Yes, God does speak. Yes, the God of scripture speaks clearly, just as clearly as He speaks throughout the Bible. There are many who disagree with me. There are those who say God speaks only through the Bible. Then there are those who insist God doesn't exist. Yet, the testament of the Bible is the testimony of a God who speaks into the lives of His people. The Bible is testimony of God working in people, in this world. To lock Him into the pages of a book is to dismiss all that the Bible says. God is speaking into the lives of people throughout this world: He spoke into our lives and we have followed, albeit falteringly.

This is a lesson we have learned, a lesson we continue to learn. Following God's word puts us at odds with the world. It often puts us at odds with church leaders. But it is the only way to find life. Debra knows this; our son knows this; and I, as weak and faithless as I often am, also know this. I had to ignore the words of doctors. I'm not saying ignore your doctors. However, I am saying, if what God tells you contradicts what the doctors have said, then stay with God and ask Him what is next. Ask Him to lead you to the right doctors, the right diagnoses, the right situation. Throughout the pages of this book, you will see God at work. You will see how He led a simple family through a story that will shock some and connect deeply with others.

God has forced me to depend on Him. He has forced me, for the sake of my family, to listen to Him, to obey Him, to walk with Him. I admit, I have not enjoyed it. I have not been easy to lead. But bit by bit God is breaking me down; He is humbling me. Now I am grateful. I'm grateful for the end of our world and the beginning of living in His.

Chapter Two

Life Beneath the Branches

Never be afraid to trust an unknown future to a known God.

- Corrie Ten Boom

The scent of pine filled the summer air as a gentle breeze wound its way through the forest, filling me with peace. It was 1989 and I was in my favorite hiding spot at Good News Camp, burrowed beneath pine needles under the low-hanging branches of just the right tree in just the right spot, waiting for the campers to give up on finding me in their favorite game of "Counselor Hunt". I was a counselor for a group of boys at the camp, on duty 24/7, so a time to rest was grasped eagerly. Awaiting the sound of "all clear", I soon fell asleep, comforted by the close embrace of the boughs and branches.

Reflecting more recently about my long-ago experiences of hiding under the pines at camp, I realized that not only was I well hidden from those searching for me, but they, and the rest of the world, were also hidden from my view. The branches provided separation from both perspectives. During those days, this comforted me. Later, as Debra's health continued to deteriorate, the branches closing in around me during this crisis were suffocating.

Branches piled on when I heard my wife's cries, her heart-wrenching screams ripping apart the night. My son's questioning looks and my inability to provide reassuring answers weighed me down, as if I was pinned under a fallen tree. The doubting looks and scoffing laughter from doctors became branches and vines wrapping around me, clinging to me, beating at me in the wind. Instead of providing comfort, the branches closing in made me feel as if I was being buried alive. They blocked my view of the rest of the world. It seemed as if I had vanished from all those around me.

After the first attempt to gain treatment, Debra's health did not improve and I watched helplessly as she suffered. At a time soon thereafter, we arrived at a specialist's office, having been recommended to him by the hospital doctors. Any hope we carried in with us was quickly shattered when the doctor arrogantly asserted, "There is nothing wrong with you! I've read the reports! I will not see you until you get an evaluation from the neuropsychologist." We had not even said one word to him. Debra tried to respond but he simply cut her off, offered me a limp handshake and walked out. I wanted to crush his little hand, among other things. Instead, I stood up and helped Debra to her feet. As we stormed out the door, I tossed the uncompleted paperwork at the startled receptionist. We would not be back.

Crushed again, we felt abandoned and alone until we remembered, God had told us Debra would be well again, not that this specialist would make her well.

Yes, God *had* spoken and he continued to speak. He spoke gently but urgently to my wife, consistently saying "1-copper, 2- _____, 3- _____, etc." We listened as God continued to tell us Debra would be well again. When people came and prayed for her healing, we told them we believed in healing, and we believed in God's ability to heal. However, we had also learned to listen and He was clearly telling us immediate, overnight healing was not what He would do in our case. Their looks of disagreement were like ice cold drops of rain added to the winds of the storm. We tenaciously held to God's word while battling anger at their stubborn misunderstanding.

After a while, we visited the Emergency Room in a neighboring town, only to be told, at first, the doctor thought Debra's illness was something psychological. "I'm a counselor!" I angrily retorted. "I work with psychosomatic illnesses. This is not psychosomatic!!" This seemed to stop him. He began to change his thinking, searching, looking for anything that might fit what he was seeing.

As we prepared to leave the ER, he looked at me and said with a fatherly concern, "I would be breaking down the door of every doctor until I found the answers!" I was grateful for his empathy, especially since I was not a forceful person and not fond of telling "experts" they were wrong. God used the doctor's words to encourage me as things got unbelievably worse.

Over the months we saw numerous doctors, all who looked at us as though we were crazy because their tests revealed nothing about Debra's illness. One doctor said that Debra was simply suffering from dry mouth! He encouraged us to get an over the counter mouth wash which would help restore the moisture in her mouth!

"What about the abdominal pain?!" my wife cried. "What about the metal taste in my mouth?! What about the fact I'm urinating every 15 minutes?" He just looked at us in confusion as I struggled to contain my anger at encountering yet another clueless physician. However, we had heard God's voice and God gave us direction- "copper". What did it mean?

We began to research anything that related to copper levels in the body. This research led us to an illness called Wilson's disease. Interestingly, we found a hospital that had a Wilson's disease clinic within a 45-minute drive of our residence. I immediately called the clinic and conversed with one of the nurses regarding symptoms. She suggested I bring Debra into the Emergency Room so tests could be run. Debra and I eagerly grabbed the opportunity and headed to the Emergency Room with hope rising.

"This time things would be different!" we thought. The physician on duty was phenomenal. The first test came back consistent with Wilson's disease. He let us know that Debra would be hospitalized in order to finish the testing. The knot in my stomach began to relax.

"Finally!" I thought, "We are finally getting somewhere."

However, this doctor was at the end of his shift. "I will be heading out shortly, but I will leave this information with the next doctor and he will get you a room to finish the testing," he explained.

Shortly thereafter we heard a voice in the hall outside our room say, "Hey! I just learned what Wilson's disease is!" The door opened, revealing a doctor who looked no more than 20 years of age. "Your wife doesn't have Wilson's disease," he began. "I'm sending her home."

At that point, I snapped. "That's not what the other doctor told me!"

He stepped back and said, "Well, we can put her in for observation."

"No!" I practically yelled, terrified they would eventually send us home with no answers. "You *will* finish the tests! That is what the other doctor ordered!" At this point, I was beyond exhausted. "I won't take her home like this! You'll have to get a social worker here!" The doctor looked at me, stunned. I won out, and at midnight they admitted Debra and collected samples all the next day. But I never saw another doctor at that hospital. Though I let the staff know when I would be arriving, the doctors managed to leave shortly before I showed up.

Finally, just before Debra was released, a young female resident came to speak with me. "We can't keep your wife unless you agree that she be moved to the neuropsych unit." she said in an anxious voice.

"Why?" I questioned. The young resident just put her head down, refusing to answer. "Why?!" I forcefully demanded.

"So they can start her on psychiatric medications," she finally admitted. I shook my head, wanting to tear the hospital apart; but I refused to take out my anger on this young intern. I declined the request to have Debra moved to the neuropsych unit, so the doctors released her, sending us home with two, 1-gallon jugs to continue collecting urine samples for the remainder of the Wilson's disease testing. Debra was discharged into a blizzard in the middle of rush hour in Ann Arbor, Michigan. Again, I was deflated, defeated, and needless to say, extremely disgusted with another dead-end experience. But our situation was to get darker. The branches were beginning to make it more and more difficult to see anything beyond our pain.

The next day we returned to the Wilson's disease clinic with the two 1-gallon jugs of collected urine. The staff at the clinic was stunned. "What is this?!" they asked.

"The urine collection you requested," we responded.

"Is this what they sent you home with?"

"Yes."

"We can't use this! Why didn't they call us?" We were dismayed. Unfortunately, the hospital staff had been collecting the urine samples in the wrong containers. I wanted to break into sobbing but tears couldn't get to the surface. We found we had been put into the middle of a squabble between doctors: the lack of respect between them was unsettling. It was also extremely time consuming as we now had to go home and collect urine samples again, this time with the right containers. Once again, however, we were left with no answers. The samples came back negative. It wasn't Wilson's disease.

Later, at the same hospital, we met with a liver specialist who told us again that there was nothing wrong with Debra's liver. "Is it possible the supplements she is taking for liver function could be masking the results of the testing?" I questioned.

"No, that's not possible," he stated firmly.

His supervisor, an extremely young doctor, came in then. "You don't need all those supplements," he spoke arrogantly. "I would stop using them immediately!"

I looked over at Debra who was sitting on the exam table. She returned my look, mirroring my own expression. I was disturbed, knowing my wife would be screaming without the supplements, knowing they were the only thing that had provided any form of comfort for her. We left the office knowing we would not return, despite their desire for follow-up.

That experience was the heaviest branch of all, at least to this point. I was done; Debra was finished. Daaron and I did as she asked, calling each person on her list and letting her say good bye to them. We didn't expect her to make it through the night. She was so weak, so frail; it seemed merciful to pray that God would take her out of her suffering.

At this point, the underside of the branches was all we could see. These branches seemed to gain weight with each passing day. We lay beneath those branches, unable to see anything beyond. But God wasn't finished with Debra. He wasn't finished with us. He hadn't given up on speaking and He certainly would not go back on his word. He was orchestrating things beyond our ability to see. Beyond our "hiding" place, God was working, moving, and connecting things that would be seen at a later time. We were learning to live in His world- to live by faith.

I would like to say we patiently rested in the hiding place beneath the pines, but in reality, we were screaming like scared children. We fought, and continue to fight, through the suffering. However, even in the midst of the tantrums and pain, we heard God's voice. We clung to God's voice. We submitted, however unwillingly, to whatever God was orchestrating above the branches, beyond our view. His wounded children were slowly being shaped into the prayer warriors He desired.

Chapter Three

Wounded Prayer Warriors

Never trust a Christian leader who does not walk with a limp.

- A. W. Tozer

Growing up, missionary biographies always inspired me. Over and over the stories of Amy Carmichael, Hudson Taylor, David Livingstone, George Muller, and others reinforced my belief that the God of the Bible still cares, still acts in the lives of His people. As a young man God drew me, calling to me through the stories of the missionaries as repeatedly I begged God to let me see Him act, just as they had. It became my desire, and still is, to prove the God of the Bible is still living and active in our lives today. And just as this faith in God put the men and women of those biographies at odds with many pastors and leaders of their day, so too I have found myself at odds with those who should have known better.

When reading as a young man it never caught my attention what this meant for the various missionaries until going through this time of seeming chaos in our own lives. God was putting me into a position of challenging the experts by simply following his will, walking in simple, though feeble faith. This has brought me to my knees, humbling me, making me, bit by bit, a wounded prayer warrior. Reluctant as I've been, I can see this is a large part of what God has been teaching me through the interaction with doctors and church leaders.

Despite the seeming incompetence of the doctors who had treated Debra, we began to see God's hand at work to bring changes. The hospital ordered home nurse visits through a home-health-care agency, which allowed us to begin the process of getting help for Debra at home.

During the first visit of the home health care nurses, assessments of Debra's condition were made. We found out later that the doctors had ordered a psychiatric nurse be included to do a mental evaluation. The nurse was disgusted, just as we were, after showing up at the home and seeing what faced her. She stated, with no uncertainty, this was not some sort of psychosomatic illness. As a matter of fact, our main nurse began writing in her notes that she feared Debra was dying and nobody was doing anything to stop it. She was distraught, and God used her to save Debra's life, perhaps at the expense of her own career.

As we prayed, I was led to call a doctor my wife had seen years before. I called him and paid for a phone consultation. After hearing the symptoms, listening to my report of the response of doctors, and asking numerous questions, he gave me the first glimmer of hope I'd had in weeks.

"It sounds to me like your wife is experiencing adrenal exhaustion or failure. Has anyone suggested this to you?" he asked.

"No." I replied, wondering what this meant.

"I'd like to send a lady who practices Jinn Shin Jyutsu." he stated. "This is an emergency and we need the body to begin to start healing on its own." He explained a little about the practice and I returned home to discuss it with my wife. As we prayed, we felt God lead us to let the practitioner begin.

That first night still impacts my memory. It was amazing! Debra's body began to relax and she fell asleep on the table as the woman's gentle fingers felt and "listened" for the body's various pulses. This began a process of twice-weekly treatments that literally seemed to bring Debra back from the brink of death. Later, when talking with the Jinn Shin Jyutsu practitioner, I realized how concerned she was after her first meeting with Debra. She confirmed what Debra had been telling me, that Debra had been near death. God had brought this person in the nick of time.

In the meantime, the doctor actually came to our house to examine Debra. He concluded she was, indeed, suffering from adrenal exhaustion. He began treating her with a variety of supplements and my wife's energy seemed to improve. However, some of the supplements made my wife's symptoms worse. When we told the doctor this, he stated, rather brusquely, that some people just don't want to get better! At that I felt my blood begin to boil once again.

27

At a later house visit, he administered a drug without asking about Debra's allergies. Within seconds, my wife went completely limp and was unresponsive. Her jaw dropped open. Her skin turned whiter than it already had been. Suddenly, she gasped for air and took a deep breath, then went completely limp again. Her oxygen levels began dropping dangerously low. The doctor looked up at me, sweat running down his forehead, and said, "Now would be a good time to start praying."

I immediately prayed against the effects of the medication, prayed for strengthening of her muscles, and prayed for oxygen levels to return to normal. I just simply prayed whatever God brought to mind while the doctor began doing everything possible in order to keep the oxygen levels up. This continued for about forty minutes, when suddenly she began to breathe normally. The doctor went out to his vehicle and brought in oxygen and began IVs for Debra. Then he looked at me and said, "That should not have happened."

"What shouldn't have happened?" I asked. In my mind I was furious. He shouldn't have given her the medication without asking about drug allergies.

He replied, "That medication doesn't get out of the system that quickly. It should have taken well over two hours." As we looked at each other, I knew full well God's spirit had flowed through Debra's body in answer to prayer, cancelling the effects of the medication.

From that point on the doctor seemed to do all he could to get out of treating Debra. Anger raged within me again. I was angry at the doctor. I was angry at Debra. I was angry at God. I was angry with myself. Yet God did not leave.

Because Debra had been connected with the home health care agency, we were able to get other help. I convinced the doctor to order IVs and oxygen for Debra since she had improved greatly while using them. I also convinced him to run a metal toxicology test. Although he did it reluctantly, and we had to pay out of pocket, we were finally able to get a true, accurate test of metal levels in my wife's body. When the results came back, we were not surprised that copper levels were high. We were, however, surprised by how high other levels of metals were.

Despite the results showing unusually high levels of metals in Debra's body, the doctor said he thought the root problem was psychological, not physical. He began to distance himself from us, not returning our phone calls. He did order oral chelation for Debra in order to begin to rid her body of the metals, but it was quite obvious things still weren't right.

Shortly thereafter, Debra said God was telling her we needed to visit a different doctor, that the current doctor was just a link in the chain and had accomplished his purpose. This revelation unleashed a fury within me. Constant exposure to skepticism, the refusals, and the accusations of doctors was too much and the anger it created began to express itself toward Debra. God was turning up the heat in the refining fire. He was beginning a work that has continued to this day. It was a work which I vigorously resisted. Fortunately, God has graciously insisted on building his prayer warriors.

Let it not be misunderstood, I am not a prayer warrior, though I always wanted to be. Until now, I had not realized what that meant. If you are a follower of Jesus, if you truly listen to God with a desire to obey, you will often stand at odds with the experts among men, both those in the church as well as those in the world.

God does not care what the experts say. He uses people who are willing to look foolish by simply saying "God said to do it this way." And sometimes, in order to reveal His glory, His leading from above, He even uses the reluctantly willing, the preacher with a limp, the weak-kneed warrior of prayer.

Chapter Four

Prayer Meeting and the Doctor

It is a sad day for righteousness when church politics instead of holy praying, shape the administration of the kingdom and elevate men to place and power.

-E. M. Bounds

Growing up, children weren't much involved in the church prayer meetings. Our church, like so many others, was under the mistaken assumption prayer was for adults. Children and teenagers were meant to be "learning" in the classroom. It seemed my parents only prayed before meals and before bed. Of course, looking back, it is easy to see this wasn't true. However, if it hadn't been for the exposure to numerous missionary biographies, the tradition of confining prayers to meal time and bed time would probably have been continued. Because of the missionary stories though, the idea of waiting on the Lord, listening in every situation, began to take root. And when Debra and I met, the root began to bear fruit.

Although it seems God was at work creating a prayer warrior through the current situation of my wife's illness, it is now obvious He'd been creating one long before our current experience. As a high school student, slips of paper containing numerous prayers littered my large bedroom desk. Begging God to speak clearly to me and asking for wisdom, the conclusion that God *was* answering me became clear. He was often simply waiting on me to act on what He was saying. This was the difficulty. *I* was the difficulty.

The first time Debra and I prayed together in college left an indelible mark on my soul. It was so powerful it scared her. She refused to pray with me for quite some time after that. When Debra and I got married it became obvious Debra was someone who made things happen through prayer. It always amazed me how she prayed and God acted. God taught me more through her than He had taught me through all the missionary stories. Finally the question was raised, "How come when you pray things happen?"

She responded "I ask God what he wants me to pray and then I pray what He tells me."

"Isn't that like asking my dad what he would like me to ask him for at Christmas?" I questioned, astonished! In my mind, prayer was still simply a time of requests, not an act of communicating with the divine.

"No!" she responded, giving me an odd look. "It is going to my master and asking him what his orders are for the day."

I sat, stunned! Yes, that certainly made sense. Isn't that what asking in Jesus' name truly means? And learning to act on what He, my master and lord desires, begins in the act of praying.

Yes, God was at work in my life, especially in the realm of prayer and its necessity for life. It was obvious every situation confronting us had been conquered or arranged by God through prayer. This is the truth for all of us, whether we are aware of it or not. Thus, on that gray April day, when the slip of paper containing the name and phone number of a doctor was given to me, it caught my attention. It came from a prayer meeting of a small church I'd never been to. Well, I should say, I grudgingly took notice. Ok, well, actually, the number was put aside like so many other pieces of advice people had given us. However, this one would not leave me alone. Especially with Debra insisting it was time to find a new doctor.

Finally, the call was made and I found myself explaining the situation, fully expecting the disbelieving responses I'd become accustomed to hearing. The woman on the other end replied "Oh, I'm sorry, but the doctor doesn't have any openings until October."

"My wife won't be alive by then!" I responded, exhausted and angry.

"Well, his nurse practitioner has an opening in May. Would you like me to schedule an appointment with her?"

"Sure," I responded, defeated. "Six weeks or six months doesn't really make a difference. I don't think she'll last. But, let's at least get her an appointment."

Resigning myself to the thought I'd done all I could was a sign of the extreme exhaustion overwhelming my family. The receptionist put me on hold while she looked for the May appointment. Suddenly she came back on the line, and in a surprised voice said "Well! She's got an opening this week! Do you want it?"

"Absolutely!" I responded.

Later that week we headed for another doctor's appointment. My enthusiasm was gone. The numerous negative visits to health professionals had taken their toll and the thought of another doctor telling us there was nothing wrong with my wife was more than I thought I could bear. Even the thought of another doctor's look of disbelief filled my mind with dread. Every mocking voice, arrogant response, rolled eye, or other disbelieving response was replayed through my mind on the long, 45-minute drive to the doctor. By the time we pulled in the parking lot my stomach was so knotted up, my shoulders so tense, it was all I could do to propel Debra into the waiting room.

As we sat in the office of the nurse practitioner I began speaking for Debra. The anger and frustration must have registered clearly on my face. Shortly after beginning, the nurse practitioner put her hand up and said to me "It's obvious your wife is sick. You don't have to convince me! Her skin, her hair, her weight all show she is sick. She is being poisoned. And the test results from this other doctor are valid and accurate." The tension seemed to fall from my shoulders. Even writing this makes my eyes water as the stress rolls off my shoulders.

"However," she continued, "there is something else going on here. Your wife never worked in a situation where she would have been exposed to

34

high levels of metal." She paused, as if in deep thought. "Have you ever been exposed to mold?" she asked suddenly.

"No." I responded without thinking.

"Yes." came the response from my wife's mouth. Turning, my jaw dropping, I looked at her as she continued. "All growing up there was mold in the corner of my bedroom where my stuffed animals were. My parents would just paint over it every year."

The nurse practitioner nodded as she said "That was common during the '70s and '80s. Most of what we've learned about mold has come since hurricane Katrina." I just nodded dumbly. "Actually, not everyone is reactive to mold. And it isn't the mold itself, it is the biotoxins. Most people's immune systems kick out the biotoxins immediately, recognizing them as toxic. However, there is a certain genetic type in which the immune system doesn't seem to recognize the biotoxins as toxic. They build up in the body until other systems start malfunctioning, causing all kinds of issues, from neurological to muscular to respiratory." I just sat there. My mind couldn't comprehend what was being said. The only thing I cared about was whether or not they could help my wife, give my son back his mom, and restore "normalcy" to our lives.

This visit left us with the gift of restored hope. This was the greatest gift that we could have received at this point: Hope. A plan was also put in place. Intravenous chelation was prescribed and begun that very week. Debra was put on the doctor's emergency cancelation list and a number of tests were also quickly scheduled.

One of these tests consisted of an on-line vision test. It was a simple test, to my mind. One simply had to look at a series of boxes with lines filling them, then indicate which direction the lines were pointing; up, right, or left. My wife sat down to take the test, read the instructions, and began looking through the samples. Tears began to fill her eyes.

"What's wrong?" I questioned.

"I don't understand." she responded.

"What don't you understand?" I asked, rather impatiently.

"How to do the test!" she said, getting angry with my impatience.

"Well, you simply look at the lines in the boxes and indicate which direction they are going." I said, reading the instructions for her.

"I can read!" she raised her voice.

"Then what's the problem?!" I responded in kind.

"There aren't any lines in the boxes." she said, pointing to the boxes in explanation.

"Um… yes… there are." I said, trying to keep my voice calm. "See here," I pointed at the first box. "These are slanted to the right." I traced the lines with my finger.

"What lines?" she asked, crying. "I don't see any!"

"Oh…." I said, letting my voice trail off.

We just looked at each other for a few moments. Excitement was rising inside! This test was meant to check for toxins in the blood stream. The poisons, having reached the brain, would make it difficult for the person to see contrast. Suddenly many things were becoming clear to me. For instance, my wife was always saying it was dark. Well, it certainly was dark for her. She despised night driving, as she couldn't see clearly. Until this moment it had never made sense to me how she had perfect vision on all her vision tests, yet complained so much of being unable to see. Things were slowly taking shape.

Yes, the excitement was beginning to energize us. Just having answers that seemed to make sense was exhilarating. As Debra began doing chelation and continued with Jinn Shin Jyutsu, we saw her begin to regain some life. The abdominal pain was slowly lessening. There was actually excitement about meeting the doctor and hearing the results of the tests. We were ready for answers, or so we thought.

As we sat in his office, the doctor looked at both of us and said, with a straight face, "You are on my top five list... And that's not a list you want to be on because I get all the crazy cases." He looked at us over the top of his glasses. I didn't know whether to laugh or cry. In that moment, with a serious expression on his face, he looked just like Jay Leno. I had to restrain myself from reacting with an emotion completely inappropriate for the moment.

"You've definitely been exposed to mold." he started. He explained the different tests carefully and slowly. "You definitely have metal toxicity but we are working on that." he continued. "And finally, this test here tells me you've got some sort of infection. We've got to figure out what's causing the infection," he finished, looking back and forth at each of us.

"Well," I offered, "There is a doctor in Jackson who just ordered a test for Lyme disease, although it has been almost two years since Debra was bit."

"That would be my first guess." He responded, shocking me. "But don't be surprised if it comes back negative. I've got another lab in California that has a better test. We'll send a sample to them if this one comes back negative."

We left his office with a prescription for pure, powdered, cholestyramine from a compounding pharmacy to begin the process of removing the biotoxins. We were to continue the chelation and see him in four to six weeks to discuss the results of the testing.

As Debra and I prayed, with thanksgiving, we asked God to give us the next step. This had become our standard prayer. He was our Lord, and we were simply trying to follow His orders. This time, as we prayed, Debra stopped me, asking "Can I tell you what I'm seeing?"

"Please." I responded.

"Remember the list?" she asked.

"Yes." I excitedly replied.

"Well, I see 1. Copper, followed by a bunch of other metals; 2. Mold; and 3. _____ disease. God is slowly filling in the list!"

It was difficult restraining myself. Knowing God was leading us was electrifying! It seemed as if we would be coming out of this soon. We found ourselves giving thanks to God, ready to go on with life. Little did we know what life had in store. Hardship was just beginning.

A few weeks later we were again in the doctor's office. He informed us both tests came back inconclusive. "The first test has three markers. In order for it to come back positive, you have to have two of the three come back positive. One marker was positive, one was negative, and one was inconclusive." He continued, "The second test has six markers, and basically there was a positive, a couple negatives, and the rest were inconclusive." The disappointment must have shown on my face. It just seemed answers were so elusive.

He wasn't finished, however. "The positive marker on both tests was the same. It tells us what kind of bacteria your body is trying to fight. It shows you are fighting spirochete bacteria and there are only two diseases you get from spirochete bacteria, at least in this part of the world. The first is Lyme disease, of which you have many symptoms. The other is a disease for which you have no symptoms. So.... it is Lyme disease." He finished, looking from Debra to myself. "Actually, it is better to call it post-Lyme syndrome. They no longer accept chronic Lyme disease. However, since it has been two years since you were bit, this makes sense."

"So, what do we do now?" I asked.

"Well, typically, we treat Lyme with a month of intravenous antibiotics. However, in your wife's state, that would kill her." He continued, "Your wife is so weak she would die if we did that. However, we can give her an oral antibiotic. It will be difficult, though."

And it was. My wife lay in bed, screaming in pain, convulsing for almost the whole month. When we went back to the doctor, I found the old fear began creeping into my gut. What would he do now, as Debra clearly didn't get better? Would he blame her, as other doctors had? Would he give up? Would we be left with no answers? My stomach was in knots again as we entered his office.

"Well," he began, after hearing our account, "We won't do that again!" The fear fell from me upon hearing this. The doctor continued "There are many ways to treat this. If you go to a conference on Lyme disease, you can hear ten different speakers who all have different ways that have been effective in treating this disease. With your wife, we are going to have to slow down. She is so toxic, so sensitive to *everything* we will have to go slow."

We left encouraged. Debra and I knew we had found our doctor. Or, it should be stated, God found our doctor. He led us through a prayer meeting; a prayer meeting in a small church where we'd never attended; a prayer meeting where the people did not know us. A woman who was willing to listen to God and obey, regardless of whether or not we ever met her or ever thanked her, connected us to this place. And God continued to remind us this person, although a great doctor, was also human. Ultimately it would be God who led us, God who healed us. We would have to follow him without wavering, even if it meant losing all. And it did.

Chapter Five

Homeless

Now it happened as they journeyed on the road, that someone said to Him, "Lord, I will follow You wherever You go." And Jesus said to him, "Foxes have holes and birds of the air have nests, but the Son of Man has nowhere to lay His head."

- Luke 9:57-58

It used to be my boast I could sleep anywhere. And it was true. As a youth leader, I took a group to an all-night event. About two o'clock in the morning, with no place to sit, no place to rest, I simply lay down on the concrete, put my face directly on its coolness, and fell asleep. I was young then, still in my twenties. Now, however, this boast was to be put to the test. Could I, or better yet, *would* I sleep anywhere God would take us? Jesus' statement, "the Son of Man has nowhere to lay His head" would become very real for my family.

As we finished up the oral antibiotics, we were heading into August. We were seeing great progress with Debra's health. Yes, she was still using oxygen, and yes, she was still on IVs twenty-four hours a day, but she was able to sleep, a little, and able to walk with a walker. The abdominal pain had decreased tremendously with the chelation. It seemed we were headed in the correct direction. As a matter of fact, towards the middle of October 2013, Debra was able to go ten days without the IVs. We were delighted! However, although she was ok without the oxygen when we were outside, as soon as we entered our home again she struggled to breathe. We would immediately hook her back up to the oxygen.

Then the leaves fell, the rain came, and all of a sudden Debra was on her back again. We began to realize how badly any kind of mold affected her. As a matter of fact, everything, every scent, every surface seemed to bother her. And not simply "bother" her, Debra would actually go into convulsions, screaming in pain.

As stated previously, we prayed about everything, and God had been teaching me to listen. Praying one day, God very clearly communicated to me to pray for a new house. This disturbed me, as God had never spoken something like this to me. Yet it was very clear. And it became clearer as the days progressed.

It went from "Pray for a new house," to "Pray for a house appropriate for your wife's needs." This idea didn't connect with me at first. Maybe God was simply telling me to get a ranch, to get Debra on one level, as I was carrying Debra up and down the stairs to use the bathroom. We had fallen twice. God wanted us in a safe place, but how?

And then, as we were praying, Debra looked at me, and with a pained expression on her face said "God is telling me I'm not going to make it another winter in this house." Anger, once again, colored my mind. It would probably be more honest to say the anger already within began to reveal itself. It was always right at the surface. Everything seemed to be crashing in on me, as if it was all my responsibility, and anger was my basic response.

"Well tell God He's just gonna have to provide a place!" I retorted in frustrated anger.

As winter approached, Debra began to have more and more problems. We approached the doctor, sharing our concerns. "You're going to have to get a place with all hard surfaces." He began. My eyes drilled holes in his head. He continued, seemingly unperturbed, "You cannot have carpet. You will have to have leather or wood furniture. Oh, and baseboard heat will be best for your wife. And you would be better on a slab, rather than a basement or crawl." Silently innumerable thoughts slammed through my mind. Finally, we asked what he thought about us finding a rental. He just shook his head. As we headed home, my prayers began to make sense.

We ended up getting rid of all fabric furniture in the home; the couches, chairs, mattresses.... everything!! Debra was moved into the only section of the house which was not carpeted, the kitchen. Daaron and I were having to cook on the front porch because the smells made Debra convulse or throw-up. It felt as if we were going backward.

In the meantime, as we prayed, we continued to hear God tell us to pray for a new house. And it was clear he was telling us a house, not an apartment. We had no money, no ability to get a mortgage, and my wife was deteriorating. Writing letters, I pleaded with fifteen different Christian organizations, laying out our circumstances and asking for help. We heard nothing back from the majority. Those we did hear from basically said "We're praying for you but we can't help you." It was devastating.

Speaking with a chaplain from a prominent Christian organization, I was simply told I needed to find a new job. The twenty hours a week of work as well as the counseling was overwhelming me as it was. It wasn't possible to be gone more often, leaving my son to care for my wife. The complete waste of time caused me to be more and more disgusted with "Christian" organizations and businesses. It was as if they had completely forgotten James chapter 2.

> What good is it, my brothers and sisters, if you say you have faith but do not have works? Can faith save you? If a brother or sister is naked and lacks daily food, and one of you says to them, "Go in peace; keep warm and eat your fill," and yet you do not supply their bodily needs, what is the good of that? So faith by itself, if it has no works, is dead.
> (James 2:14-17)

My next contact, a place in Florida where they set us up with a group from Grand Rapids, Michigan, was at least willing to pay the first month's rent on an apartment for us. But again, we knew God was telling us we could not move into an apartment. And then, as we prayed, God said "Pray for a new car." This was too much! I had to be hearing wrong. However, I continued to pray. And I did, however unwillingly, pray for a house and a car.

And then, at the end of December, the 29th actually, my wife simply fell apart. Her body began decompensating, rejecting everything. She had numerous bouts of diarrhea. Calling our doctor, we were told to take her to the dreaded emergency room. Debra and I had told each other we would not go back to any emergency room, for any reason. This time, however, we had a doctor, our doctor, ordering us to go. We prayed as we drove her to the ER.

My fears were put to rest as the nurse walked in, took one look at me, and said "Mr. Rogers! How are you doing?" Looking into the eyes of one of my former students comforted me; this student would take great care of my wife. And she did not let me down. They quickly concluded Debra had pneumonia and would need to be hospitalized. Debra and I were shocked, as we'd had no indication of pneumonia. However, my wife was so weak, so dehydrated, so defeated she put up no fight and we had her admitted to the hospital. At this point exhaustion overwhelmed, so saying goodbye to Debra, I headed home.

By this time, as I've said previously, we had no furniture left in the house. Daaron and I were sleeping in the same room, on the floor, and as soon as our heads hit the pillows we were asleep. Around 2 am the phone next to my head began ringing.

"Hello?" I answered, rather groggily.

"Hello. Mr. Rogers? This is your wife's nurse at the hospital. I'm calling to let you know we're moving Debra to the critical care unit. Her oxygen levels continue to drop and we are going to have to put her on a ventilator."

"Do I need to come in?" I questioned, completely awake now.

"No. I don't think that'll be necessary. I just wanted to let you know."

"Ok, thank you." Hanging up the phone, I began to lay my head back on my pillow, and then sat up. "God," I began praying, "Should I go in while they move my wife?"

Before the prayer was even finished, the phone rang again.

"Hello?"

"Hi. This is the nurse again. I think maybe you should come down here."

"I'll be there shortly!" I said, hanging up the phone before shaking my head in disbelief. God continued to amaze me. Waking Daaron up, I let him know what was going on, and then honored his request to let him sleep.

My wife was already in the critical care unit by the time I arrived, but the doctors and nurses had run into a problem. "We need to put a pic line in," they explained. "She is going to be on a ventilator and will need to be fed intravenously." I nodded, understanding, as we already had a pic line in for her IVs. "The problem is," they continued "We can't put it in the arm she already had it in." They had already had to remove it from the right arm, but I still wasn't sure what the problem was. I knew there were usually three veins in each arm in which they could insert a pic line. I just returned a blank stare.

"Her other veins are too small," they said, looking at me, "Which means we need to put it in the other arm."

"Ahhh…." I said silently, as I nodded my head in understanding. To this point they had said they could not insert a pic into the left arm because of Debra's pacemaker. Until now, no one had realized the veins typically used to insert a pic were too small in Debra. This only left us with one vein in each arm. We needed the pic, but our only choice was the left arm, which meant dealing with certain risks associated with her pacemaker. I had to sign a number of papers before they finally took Debra to insert the pic and put her on the ventilator.

I walked into the small, empty, silent waiting room and soaked in the stillness. I was weary beyond reckoning. Even writing this, with almost six years gone by, I feel weariness overcoming my bones, making it difficult to continue. And yet, I know beyond any question, God saved Debra's life that night. Because Daaron and I were sleeping upstairs while Debra slept downstairs in the kitchen, Debra's oxygen levels would have dropped through the night and we would never have known until waking the next morning. We would have lost my wife. We are so grateful for God's intervention and His convincing us the ER would be ok.

It was now December 30th. Another holiday in the hospital, as Debra spent New Year's Eve and the next eight days hospitalized. She remained on a ventilator for four days. Daaron and I "celebrated" the New Year in the waiting room, although, with her being unresponsive on a ventilator, I did take Daaron to see *The Hobbit* at the local cinema on New Year's Eve. This was the extent of our celebration.

In the meantime, the thought, the words Debra told me kept filling my mind. "God is telling me I'm not going to make it another winter in this house!" They were filling my mind because I knew it was true. How could I take her home, knowing it would send her back to the hospital or kill her? Before I go on I want to make it clear, it would have been like this with almost any house we lived in. It wasn't specifically that house, but the fact there was carpeting, it was an old house with a basement, and there had been water damage at one point. It was the combination of my wife's Lyme disease, her previous exposure to mold, and the metal toxicity which made it impossible to live in almost any house. We were to find this out soon enough.

I began frantically searching, praying for a place to take her. I talked to my boss, only to be told my wife didn't meet the age requirement for the health center. I talked to the social worker, again, to no avail. This went on until the last day, the last hour even. In desperation I called a person I hardly knew who had said she had a house that was all wood floors and she would be willing to have Debra stay there. Little did she know, little did we know, what this would entail. We never went back to the house we'd lived in.

One week turned into two. Two weeks turned into a month. One month turned into an agonizing year. That's right, one year to the day Debra was hospitalized, we were basically homeless. We spent seven long months in the first person's home. It was long for them, as they gave up much to have us living with them. It was long for us, as my wife's health continued to deteriorate. It was long, as people often did not understand our decisions. Our decisions came from God. God led us every step, but I often could not explain God's plan to those around me. Even when explaining to Christians, other believers, what God was telling us, I was confronted with the rolled eyes, the unbelief, and the disconcerting anger. I was learning, yet again, to walk with God, despite what anyone thought or said. I was put in a position where I *had* to do this or I would lose my family.

This was the year we had nothing. Yet, we walked with God. *We* had nothing, but *God* provided everything. As I stated earlier, we spent six and a half months with our first family. Then, upon finding a house which we could buy, but needing to do some work on it, we moved an hour north to stay, what we thought would be one to two weeks, with a friend from college. He had recently built a house with all wood floors which also had a bedroom with hospital beds and a handicapped accessible bathroom. This turned into four and a half months, the end of which we were told, the week of Christmas, we had to be out by the 29th. One year to the day Debra had been hospitalized.

The house God had led us to, which we were buying on a land contract, was not ready to live in yet. There was no running water, no toilets, no stove, nothing. We moved my wife in, December 29th, 2014, and slept on the floor. Debra slept on the floor, in the middle of construction, hooked up to an IV. My beautiful, sick, hurting wife was forced to use a bucket to urinate in during the night. She had Lyme disease, metal toxicity, and extreme allergies to mold, and I watched, torn up, as I had no place to offer her true rest. Daaron and I slept on the floor as well. Daaron and I slept on the floor for over a year. And it broke my heart.

It also made me think of Jesus' statement, "Foxes have holes and birds of the air *have* nests, but the Son of Man has nowhere to lay *His* head." I used to think he said this condemningly, knowing the man would not follow. And maybe, in one sense, this is true. But I now see things from the point of view of a husband and father who has had to watch his wife and son literally have nowhere to lay their heads. It ripped my heart to shreds. It is one thing for me to have these things happen, to have no place of my own in which to lay my head. But to see my loved ones go through this broke me. I would have wept, but I had become so hardened that I simply plowed on. However, I believe it also broke Jesus, as he knew, he could see, what his loved ones would be put through on this earth. He has shown me both sides, both views of this particular saying. And he has filled me, or is trying to empty me so he can fill me, with *His* passion for his family. And I, many times unwillingly, follow the One who has nowhere to lay His head.

But I've gotten ahead of myself. We were still living with others. We were still praying, asking, struggling, and arguing with the God of the universe; the God of the universe whose son had nowhere to call his own. There was much to learn before we found a home of our own.

Chapter Six

Red Chariot

God is not a man, that He should lie; neither the son of man, that He should repent: when He hath said, will He not do it? or when He hath spoken, will He not make it good?

- Numbers 23:19

"God, you told us to pray for a house that would meet Debra's needs," we prayed. "And now we desperately need to find one. We can't stay here forever. Please, God, show us what's next." We sat quietly, listening, trying to rest in His presence. My wife sighed in frustration. This time I was sure I knew why.

"Have you picked out a car?" God seemed to reply.

I knew I had heard this, but when my wife sighed in frustration, turned to me and said "He keeps saying "Have you picked out a car?"", I knew beyond a doubt. How frustrating, infuriating even.

"God," we cried out again, "We need a house that fits Debra's needs!"

And again, God responded with, "Have you picked out a car?"

We were flabbergasted! Here we were, living in someone else's home, desperately in need of a place of our own where Debra could heal, and every time we prayed, God would direct us back to the issue of picking out a car. While I didn't tell Debra, I spent a lot of time arguing with God over this.

"God, we are living in someone else's home. We can't stay here. Why would you tell us to look for a car when we desperately need to get out of their home?" I would argue.

"It's not their home." God would reply.

"Okay. And I'm supposed to tell them this?"

"No. You don't have to. It's not for you to say."

"Then what, God? How am I supposed to do this?"

"Just pick out a car."

"I can't just do that!"

"Why not?"

My response to this question revealed the crux of the problem. The problem was me. My pride interfered with so much of what God wanted to do. You see, I was worried about how it would look. How would people perceive me? What would be said if I took what money I did have and bought a nice vehicle? I couldn't stand the thought of other people thinking, saying, or asking things for which I had no response. Well, I had a response,

52

just not one I felt comfortable telling people. I mean, it is one thing to be-lieve God speaks, and speaks clearly if we listen. It is another thing, in our secular society, to tell people you are doing something simply because "God told me to." And…. I was afraid. Fear drove me then and has continued to hinder my relationship with God, Debra, and Daaron.

"Okay God," I began arguing again, "so I tell everyone you told me to do it. What then?" I expected God to answer with understanding and comfort, saying something to let me know He understood how unreasonable I thought He was being.

Instead, we just kept hearing "Have you picked out a car?" Finally, I gave in, reluctantly, angrily, in utter frustration. I knew God was guiding, so in spite of my fear, Debra and I began the process of picking out a vehicle. The first thing we did was consult with our doctor.

"It will have to have a leather interior." He began.

"Ok. What else?"

"It cannot be brand new. The fumes would kill her."

"And?"

"It can't be over two to three years old because it will have picked up mold in the carpeting."

"Ok…." I wasn't sure what to say or do. I knew we were in trouble. I knew the car I had was causing Debra incredible discomfort and making her convulse and scream in pain the entire time we were using it. We had begun borrowing vehicles with leather interiors so I could take Debra to her ap-pointments. It just wasn't acceptable to drive 50 miles one way to go to an appointment where they were trying to rid Debra's body of toxins while sitting in a car full of mold both ways. I could see God was right, but I wasn't happy about it. My fear, fed by my pride, continued to make this dependence on God a difficult way of life.

We began looking at a local car dealership for vehicles to meet Debra's needs. I went to them, explained our situation, explained my wife's illness to the best of my ability, and asked them what they could do. I knew I couldn't get a loan. I knew I needed to pay cash. I also knew it was possible I might get a significant amount from a fund for employees with catastrophic needs at my place of employment. I began shopping on faith.

The car dealership began by sending us home in a fully loaded Buick Regal, leather interior, one year old. They told me to take the car home, drive my wife in it for a while, and let them know. It was at this time that other issues facing my wife came to the forefront. She had been in an automobile accident years before where she had numerous injuries which were now making it difficult for her to be comfortable in many vehicles. Her height of 5 feet, combined with the injuries, combined with the current illness, combined with the angle of head rests in new vehicles, was making things seemingly impossible.

This first vehicle, although beautiful, wasn't going to work. We next went to a scaled down Buick Regal, again, about a year old. At first, we thought it would work. However, I began thinking about the long ride back and forth to Ann Arbor twice a week, and decided to test it out on a similar trip. One trip was enough to tell me Debra would not be able to ride in comfort in this vehicle. This began a process of testing vehicle after vehicle.

Finally, when I was ready to give up, the dealership asked me to come back and try one more vehicle. It was the same brand as one we had previously tried. The previous vehicle had been comfortable for my wife but it was obvious the previous owner had been a smoker and when Debra sat in the car she immediately went into convulsions. I left Debra at "home" as I went to pick up another test vehicle.

Debra, in the meantime, was having a frank conversation with God. "Am I even going to find one that will work?" she asked.

"It will be the red one." she heard.

"Ummm......God.... I'm not going to tell Mike to take a vehicle back because it isn't the right color!"

He simply responded again, "It will be the red one."

Meanwhile, I had arrived at the dealership and was shown to a beautiful, 2013 Chevy Impala, with a black leather interior. It had about 30,000 miles on it and would be available at the same price as any of the others we had attempted. Although it was beautiful inside, I wasn't thrilled with the exterior color. However, I wasn't going to argue. "The color doesn't matter anyway," I thought.

I got in and headed back to Debra and Daaron. It was a beautiful drive, I must admit. As I pulled in the driveway I was praying that this vehicle would work and that we would somehow come up with the money to cover the cost. Walking into my wife's room, she looked up at me and asked, rather timidly, "What color is it?"

Although stunned by the question, I somewhat disgustedly said "It is a bright red." I was going to continue with how I didn't like the color but before I could say anything else Debra burst into tears. We went out to the vehicle, got in, and went for a drive. I still didn't know why she was crying, but as we drove she shared her story. My mouth dropped in astonishment. The car fit her perfectly. The interior was clean and she could literally sleep in it. And, not only that, it was the bright red God had told her it would be.

Amazingly, by the end of the week, we had been given more than enough needed to purchase the car outright. I went into the dealership, wrote out the largest check I'd ever written, and walked out with a bright red, all leather interior, 2013 Chevy Impala. God had supplied. We had heard God speak, we had grudgingly obeyed, and we were rewarded with our bright red chariot, a constant reminder of the blood Jesus shed to cover our sins, to shield us from death, to bring healing and wholeness to the sick and suffering. A reminder that the God of the universe keeps His word.

Chapter Seven

Giving and Receiving Correct Counsel

I claim the holy right to disappoint men in order to avoid disappointing God.

–A. W. Tozer

"You need to learn how to take counsel!" The pastor began, in his thick British accent. Looking from the pastor to the two elders in his office, a feeling of deep disappointment and anger began to boil over within me. This meeting had been arranged by the pastor of the church where Daaron had been attending youth group. One of the elders arrogantly nodded in agreement with the pastor's initial assessment, while the other elder, the husband of Debra's best friend, sat with his head down. We were seated in the pastor's office, as he had invited me in to "see how we can help you."

Debra had been extremely excited when I got the invitation. She was desperately hoping to have an end in sight, to have her pain, her burden, picked up and carried by a church family. I had been less optimistic, having been disappointed by so many of my previous meetings with various community pastors. I was already at a point where I wanted never to speak to another pastor.... ever. And we were just getting started.

"You need to learn to take counsel," the pastor stated again. This would have stunned me had God not been preparing me for this meeting. As it was, a sense of boldness came over me, a boldness I had not been known for.

As the pastor came around his desk, words began to flow from my mouth. "I have five people in my life that I meet with or talk to regularly. Four of them are pastors. I have no problem taking counsel from those who have taken the time to get to know me."

The pastor brushed off the comment, continuing on. It was obvious he was unaccustomed to being resisted. "We don't believe your doctor," he stated, as if the matter was settled. He continued on, letting me know the church was planning on sending Debra to "Mayo Clinic in Cleveland." When I asked if he meant Cleveland Clinic, he responded "They're the same thing." In my mind I thought back to a conversation I'd had with a woman from the church who was known in the community for stirring up trouble. It was as if her words were being spoken through the mouth of the pastor. I shook my head incredulously, thinking "Here we are without a home, living with someone else, needing a safe environment for my wife to heal and this is your counsel?!" I was stunned into silence.

Finally, feeling a sense of defeat, yet somehow emboldened, words began to tumble out of my mouth. The story of the prayer meeting which had led us to our current doctor, the account of God's provision of our current "red chariot", the reminder of this pastor's previous words, in which he agreed with my course of action, flowed from my tongue.

But the accounts of God's guidance and provision fell on deaf ears. The pastor was intent on dictating the terms of our relationship. When faced with my refusal to accept their "help", the meeting was closed with a "word of prayer" in which two of the three lectured me as they "prayed" to the very God to whom they appeared oblivious. Walking out to my waiting son was difficult, as he had grown to respect this pastor a great deal. It was the first of many disappointments for Daaron. I remember the look on Daaron's face as he asked me "How is that going to help us get a home?" As I write, I feel the pain and anger, as well as sadness because of the blessing this church missed. Its pastor was too busy dictating terms rather than leading as a servant. I'm sure, however, God is transforming his life as he has mine.

As time has gone on, God has reminded me of all the ways He has been transforming my life, especially in the area of giving and receiving counsel. Getting the right counsel *is* extremely important. *Giving* counsel without seeking God's wisdom is dangerous and extremely damaging to all involved. And counsel given from the perspective of "God no longer speaks", is simply the blind leading the blind. This is why God has taken so much time to show me the truth about counsel. And, partly, why He was breaking me.

Considering the high level of respect shown me in the past by my home church, the leadership position granted me at Good News Camp, and the quickly garnered respect of a new church as a sophomore in college, this lesson was difficult for me to accept. It felt as if my counsel to others would always be valued and accepted. This was before God began the painful process of breaking me.

Although prayers for God's will in breaking me began in 2004 and 2005, the process actually began in 1998, my first year as a music teacher. This was our family's first time beginning a search for a new family in Christ. It didn't take long to realize how truly insignificant I seemed to those around me. God took me through an extremely humbling time, a time of becoming invisible, insignificant. As we searched for a new church home, a home close enough to my place of employment, I began to feel, for the first time in my adult life, like a complete outsider. It didn't matter how many churches we attended, it just seemed as if we didn't belong, didn't fit in. Almost twenty years later I still feel this way.

And it wasn't, as many pastors like to believe, because of a lack of effort on our part. When hearing pastors say things such as, "If anyone is feeling unconnected, it is their fault. They are not making the effort to connect", my hackles get raised. No, we attempted to get involved. It is our nature. Involvement in the worship team, leadership, boards, small groups and Sunday school were commonplace to each of us. Non-involvement wasn't an option. And yet, it seemed we didn't have the right bloodlines. We were doomed to be outsiders and seemingly would never be accepted. Yet God wasn't finished.

In 2005, while praying, God asked me if I would be willing to remain completely unknown. He seemed to say "Are you willing to be nobody? Are you willing to be passed over, rejected, even spurned for my sake and the sake of your family? Are you willing to be insignificant?" This question haunted me. It still haunts me, over ten years later. Would I be willing to be non-existent? Yet, this question is the crux of the issue for all who would follow Christ.

The apostle Paul states, in his letter to the Galatians, chapter two, verse 20,

> "I have been crucified with Christ; it is no longer I who live, but Christ lives in me; and the *life* which I now live in the flesh I live by faith in the Son of God, who loved me and gave Himself for me."

In John 3:30 we hear John the Baptist state, "He must become greater and greater, and I must become less and less." This is the beginning of the life of following Christ. Life is not about us, but about pointing to the one who died for us. Life is not about our exploits, but about the exploits of the God who created us. Therefore, Jesus is everything, we are nothing. The call to insignificance, to invisibility, to being nothing, is the call of Christ. It is the call that says "Come and die." It is this call which allows us to more easily decide which counsel should be accepted and which should be declined. It is from this voice, this call, all counsel should flow.

If Jesus Christ is everything and we are nothing then all counsel is judged by Jesus, not us. All counsel is given by His spirit, the Holy Spirit. As one walks with Jesus, one becomes less and less aware of his or her own needs and desires, less aware, even, of the desires of those around them, and more and more cognizant of the desires of God rising up in them. It is through this awareness of God working in us through the Holy Spirit that all counsel is given and received. This position, this brokenness, is, I believe, only achieved in suffering. As we suffer, we are broken by God. Yet in our brokenness He, and He alone, binds our broken places, heals our wounds, dries our tears, and gives us life through death.

As we give and receive counsel, we must remember it is God who is our counselor. The Holy Spirit is given to counsel us. Unfortunately, we have little time for listening. Therefore, we tend to make principles out of scripture, force God to remain in the box we've created for Him, and claim anything beyond this is heresy. Yet, we have been given the example of Christ. Yes, we are to study the Bible. Yes, we are to memorize scripture. Yes, we are to pray. Yes, we are to meet with other believers. But in all of this we need to be still long enough to truly listen and obey the counsel of the God who still speaks. As we listen to the counsel of the Holy Spirit, we can say with A. W. Tozer "I claim the holy right to disappoint men in order to avoid disappointing God."

Chapter Eight

God's Sovereignty

You will not enter and occupy the land I swore to give you. The only exceptions will be Caleb son of Jephunneh and Joshua son of Nun. You said your children would be carried off as plunder. Well, I will bring them safely into the land, and they will enjoy what you have despised. But as for you, you will drop dead in this wilderness. And your children will be like shepherds, wandering in the wilderness for forty years. In this way, they will pay for your faithlessness, until the last of you lies dead in the wilderness.

-Numbers 14:30-33, New Living Translation

"One thing I've learned," the voice droned on "is that God's timing is perfect. We may not like it, but we simply need to be patient." The hair on the back of my neck began to stand on end. My teeth clenched as the person on the other end of the line finished her lecture. I shared the story of Joshua and Caleb, asking if it was God's will when the Israelites died in the desert. She was quiet, refusing to answer.

While God's sovereignty is real, too often people in our churches use His sovereignty as an excuse for disobedience. Please understand, this is said by me in the knowledge that my own faithlessness and its consequences would destroy me if not for God's grace and mercy extended through Jesus Christ.

However, God's sovereignty is not to be presumed upon. It is not to become an excuse for our lack of faith, our lack of action. The story of Joshua and Caleb is one of my favorites. It is remarkable in what it has to teach us; especially those who claim to bear the name of Christ. These lessons have become painfully clear as I look back over the difficult circumstances of the last six years. So, what are those lessons, and how have they been viewed through the lens of this insignificant person's struggle? God's sovereignty does not give us an excuse to disobey God, ignore other's struggles, or walk according to the flesh.

First, faithlessness and disobedience have consequences. When we use God's sovereignty as an excuse to disobey God, the consequences affect, not just ourselves, but those around us. Our story makes this painfully clear. Actually, many parts of our story poignantly drive this point into the heart. Let me share just a sampling of these stories.

The man was dying and he knew it. As I visited him in the hospital room, he looked at me, and in a ragged voice said "Mike, I told my son he is to help you in any way you need!"

"Thank you!" I replied, taken aback. This man was wealthy and had previously confided how he had stepped on many people to get the things he desired.

"I've never loved anyone," he had confessed. "Not even my wife!" Now, having heard numerous sermons from me about God's love, God's desire to love through His children, and our freedom found through loving God and loving others, this man confided in me that he was finding, after years of hurting people and caring only for himself, he couldn't simply "turn it on". I sadly commiserated with him but then was able to share that it was God's gift. He could never do it himself. This wonderful gentleman accepted God's gift and now he was dying.

The man's son, who was waiting for me in the hospital cafeteria, was wealthy as well, and childless. Sitting there, with the man who had confessed, who had previously put his trust in Jesus, I was informed he had told his son to help us with whatever we needed.

Joining the son, I sat across from him and answered his questions regarding our situation. Telling him everything, every need, every situation, was extremely difficult. As a man who believes in his abilities to take care of any situation, these conversations were a blow to my pride; they were crushing my ego. I felt small, unwanted, a nuisance. Ultimately, I became aware of my absolute insignificance. This was a beginning conversation, however, and I still felt hopeful that as I obeyed God, He would take me to others who would be obedient as well. It was the beginning of the end of that hope, however.

Although the conversation and the prayer time with my wife and son left me full of hope, in the end I was disappointed as my elderly friend died and we heard not a word from his son. His son chose to disobey his father's wishes, and we were damaged by that disobedience. Just as the Israelites suffered because they chose to follow the disobedient suggestions of the ten faithless spies, we suffered because of the disobedience of this one man. According to many, this was simply God's will.

At a later point, as we struggled against hopelessness, another man sat in his wheelchair, across from my wife, having listened to her faith and having argued with her regarding her relationship with Jesus. Finally, he forcefully stated, "Do you want to know why I don't believe?!" Turning, he pointed to the church across the street from the McDonald's where they were sitting. Jabbing his finger in the church's direction, he practically spat the words, "Here you sit, suffering, in pain, in tremendous need, and that church over there has the ability to end your suffering like that!" He snapped his fingers for emphasis. "And what have they done?"

My wife told me later, she just sat there shaking her head. As I write, I feel a furious anger with how the disobedience of church leaders has impacted the believers and unbelievers around them. I cannot be convinced this was God's will. Disobedience is a choice. It is a choice too often made by those of us who are called to be God's light in dark places. In these situations where we are called to be a light but choose to disobey we make the darkness a physical entity, we make the burden unbearable, and we make hope disappear. And, as I write, I stand condemned of so much of the same. God forgive me.

A second lesson from our story, corresponding to the story of Joshua and Caleb, is this: We cannot ignore the struggles of others all the while claiming God's sovereignty. Throughout our journey, hope would become suppressed, almost disappearing, as time after time we would obey God, share our burden with another group of believers, only to be disappointed by silence, denial, or unfulfilled promises.

My wife became suicidal. She actually attempted to take her own life several times. Later, conversing with my son I was dealt another blow which sucked the breath right out of my lungs when he informed me he had thought of numerous ways to end his life. It felt as if I'd been kicked in the groin. I wanted to curl into a ball and simply sob. And then anger overtook me and I wanted to do bodily harm to those leaders who acted as if we didn't exist. What would those who said, "It is just a matter of God's timing" while completely ignoring our desperate need, say if my wife had actually taken her own life? Or what would have been the response had I lost my son? Unfortunately, my son was probably right when he said "I couldn't end it though, dad, because I knew everyone would blame you."

If I had any tears left to cry they would be flowing freely right now. The anger often simmers below the surface as I grapple with showing mercy and forgiveness to those whose inaction and disobedience almost, and could still, cost me the lives of those I love the most. Would it have been God's will, God's timing? I think not. God's sovereignty can never be an excuse to ignore the needs of those around us.

Finally, we can never use God's sovereignty as an excuse for walking in the flesh. An example of this is actually seen in the response of many of our church leaders. One of the "favorite" responses received from church leaders was "It's just too overwhelming!" This became an excuse for doing nothing. This is a perfect example of walking in the flesh and blaming inaction on God's sovereignty. It is not God's sovereignty that causes a church leader to do nothing! It is one of a number of carnal responses.

"I can't do that for you! If I did that for you I'd have to do that for everyone."

"That is just too much!"

"You want us to have your kind of faith and that's just not going to happen!"

Each of these is a carnal response, which Jesus condemned in his first followers, by the way. When I speak to various churches, I share the story of Jesus' feeding of the five thousand. In it the disciples are challenged by our Lord to put their complete faith in His ability. They are told to do something that is an absolute impossibility in the flesh. They asked Jesus to send the crowd away so they could purchase their own food. Jesus' response amazes me.

Without batting an eye, He said "you feed them." I wonder if they thought any of the things I've been told by church leaders. Actually, we don't even have to wonder as the scripture tells us in the gospel of John, that Philip replied, "Two hundred denarii worth of bread is not sufficient for them, that every one of them may have a little." In the New Living Translation, it says, "Even if we worked for months we wouldn't have enough money to feed them!" It is a good thing Jesus didn't agree with them. We would have been left with the story of our current church in the United

States, at least those I have been presented with. Instead, however, his disciples did as he commanded, brought what little they had, put it in his hands, and Jesus mutiplied it beyond imagination. Oh what God would do in our lives if we truly entered into His kingdom living. Then, and only then, would we truly understand His sovereignty.

It is unfortunate too many of our church leaders have simply used God's sovereignty as a means of avoiding the faith to which God calls us. The lesson learned by this insignificant man is God's sovereignty does not give us an excuse to disobey God, ignore other's struggles, or walk according to the flesh. I am ashamed I have so often done each of these things. God, forgive me, forgive us, and help us walk in an obedient faith.

Chapter Nine

Stripped Naked and Spitting in the Face of God

If any man thinks ill of you, do not be angry with him, for you are worse than he thinks you to be.

-C. H. Spurgeon

Before this trial I would not have agreed with Spurgeon's words. I truly believed I was a good man. Certainly I wasn't perfect, but I was better than most. Even others told me this. But God couldn't leave me with these false beliefs. He insisted on heating me beyond my boiling point.

This boiling point was not reached immediately. It was a gradual, bit by bit, heating of the furnace of affliction. Each time I was confronted with ridicule, I would shove the resulting anger down, knowing it couldn't possibly be released. I was too righteous to give full vent to the rage fomenting within. Being forced to live in someone else's home served to put a stopper in this bottle of rage. Inside, the rage built, growing each time I was forced to beg for help. Every rejection, especially from those in the church, added heat to the fire.

Looking back, I'm reminded of the weight valve on top of the vent of a pressure cooker. I would wobble back and forth, steam pouring out but not truly released. As the heat turned up, day after day, month upon month, year upon year, the rage finally exploded, revealing who I truly was; the person only God had seen. And I was nowhere as righteous as I had believed all these years.

"I hate you!!!! I wish you were dead!" Those words flung at my wife were nothing to what came next. I can't even bear to write what happened after these words spewed from my mouth. The anger and rage raced to the surface in words and actions I would not have thought possible from me. I, after all, am a patient man. Godly is a word I've heard used of me. I've been told what a great listener I am, what a wonderful counselor. My communication skills have been complemented so often I began to believe what people were feeding me. However, the suffering, the stress of this time was beyond anything I had ever experienced. I was in the fire, the fire of purification found in the furnace of affliction. The furnace of affliction brings the dross to the surface, heats us beyond what we can bear, and leaves us naked before God. And oh how I wish this had been a one time occurrence. Unfortunately it occurred more times than I care to count. But God.... He had to remove the filth, the dross in order to see his reflection in his hurting child.

Dross. It doesn't sound so bad, dross. But read the definitions and the word becomes nauseating. In the dictionary the words "scum", "worthless", and "rubbish" are used. Synonyms include "junk", "garbage", and "trash". If someone were to call me these things, I would be furious. Or I would have been. It doesn't take much for me to see the truth. Well, just ten years of trials. I may be a little stubborn. The truth is, in myself I will find all manner of evil. One finds how true the statement, "There, but for the grace of God, go I" is of each and every one of us. And this is the place we all must go if we are to truly follow Jesus. It is in the furnace of affliction that the dross comes flowing to the surface. I truly thank God for loving me enough to take me through this purifying process. I pray He heals my family from all my sin.

The scum that came to the surface during this seemingly endless trial was, and is, nauseating. I was, and am, disgusted with myself. I should be better than this! But the words, the cursing, screaming, arguing, kicking, hitting, spitting, and throwing things are horrendous in my own eyes. And the emotional scars on Debra and Daaron are beyond what I can endure. I came to hate myself and my seeming inability to control these things which seemed to flow endlessly. The dross which was brought to the surface was ugly! Indeed, it is worthy to be called scum!

The dross doesn't end with the actions mentioned above, however. There were attitudes which became visible as well. For much of this time Debra's illness, if not Debra, was blamed for these expressions of rage. After all, it

72

Debra hadn't gotten sick we wouldn't have lost everything, been homeless, suffered ridicule, or become beggars. And if I hadn't been put in the positions mentioned above, I wouldn't be struggling like this, right? Yeah… right. Jesus endured all of this and more, yet never responded in rage. He didn't use the things He endured as reasons to sin. And He is the one I claimed to follow. God forgive me. I thought much better of myself than anyone ought. Again, God forgive me!!

See, this needs to be shared. So far, this book has dealt with lessons I've learned regarding the behavior of others and its impact on my family. However, I must turn to the even darker times, the disgusting filth flowing forth from my own heart. In my heart, in my flesh, there is nothing good. People called me patient and Godly, and I believed them. The furnace of affliction, however, reveals what is truly in the heart. It heats us beyond what we can bear in order to show us the dross within. And it was more than I could handle.

Anyone who says, "God doesn't give us more than we can handle", hasn't truly read God's word. God continually gives us more than we can handle until we get to the point where we are dead to ourselves and alive unto Him, completely dependent on Him for everything. He put me into the furnace, and it didn't take long for the dross to rise to the surface, overflowing and flowing out. I say flowing out, not seeping, because my heart was full of the very same garbage for which I so often judged others. In being heated beyond what I could bear, the things I wouldn't bear in others were revealed in myself. And it was maddening.

The furnace of affliction didn't end with simply heating me beyond my boiling point. It stripped me completely naked, both literally and figuratively.

"You stink! You know those clothes bother me! Why do you do that to me?!" Debra yelled, shaking in pain.

"I don't do anything to you!!!! I'm so sick and tired of this b*** s***!!!" I screamed at her! "Fine!", I continued, "I won't wear anything then!!!" I ripped off my sweat shirt, stripped myself of my pants, and strode completely nude to the front door. Opening it wide I threw my shredded clothes out into the rain. Turning, I screamed obscenities and spit at her as I walked out of the living room and entered the room where Daaron and I slept. Daaron looked up from where he was sitting on the floor, saw his completely naked father, looked down, and shook his head in unbelief. I shake my head in unbelief as I write this, tears seeping from my eyes. The flames of affliction had truly left me naked and spitting in the face of God.

When I was completely honest with myself, I had to admit I wasn't this fabulous person everyone had made me out to be. When Jesus said "I tell you, whatever you did to one of the least of these My brethren, you did it to Me", he is surely including my immediate family. When I cursed and spit at my wife, I was cursing and spitting in the face of Jesus. O God, please forgive me!

I used to truly believe I would never have been one of those spitting on Jesus, mocking Him, crucifying Him. That kind of behavior would not ever be tolerated in me. And yet, this is who I found underneath all the false clothing I'd managed to wear for so long. It is amazing what we can come to believe of ourselves. We resent anything bad said about us, about our character. Yet, when we get to the point of truly seeing ourselves as we are, as God sees us, we come to a place of complete contentment in Jesus. It doesn't matter what others say or think of us. We can still love and bless them because, indeed, others do not know the half of the evil we are capable of apart from the love of Jesus poured into, through, and now out of us.

Just as I stripped off my clothes, spat at my wife, and was seen walking naked through my house by my son, God has stripped me of everything revealing the complete and utter ugliness of my heart. God took me through the furnace of affliction, brought me face to face with the depth of my poverty and need, exposing the dross and ugliness, heating me beyond all I could endure, and left me crying out, naked before the Lord.

Chapter Ten

In His Hands

*But God can only smile because only God can know what is coming
next.*

- Desmond Tutu

I lay before God, naked, ashamed, and completely at the end of myself.
In this state, God began calling me to the utter and complete death of myself
in order to be resurrected by His life, His spirit within me. This teaching
had already begun, and as is often the case, God taught me intellectually and
then took me through the experience to fix the lesson within my heart.

The experiential transformation began with a missionary to the Philip-
pines. I had met him one time, earlier in my life. Amazing stories were being shared about what God had done in and through him. A friend of mine

began sending me devotionals written by this missionary. As I would read each one, my heart would leap and I would long for what I was reading. Stories of healings, miracles, and incredible workings of God would speak truth into my heart, the truth of what God's life in a dead man would do. During one Sunday service, I shared one of these devotionals with my congregation. After the service the pianist came to me saying, "You know, this man lives in the town you live in."

"What?!" I stammered.

"Yes," she replied, "he has been there for the last year."

I was speechless! Immediately I contacted the missionary, asking him for a meeting.

It was Thursday morning, March 15, 2018, that we met for over four hours. Complete transformation began at that moment. I poured out my heart, my life, and my story before him. He listened, asked questions, and then stunned me with the following statement. "I could come and pray for your wife right now and she would be healed through Jesus. However, there is a stronghold over your family and you need to do the work of getting rid of it."

"How do I do this?", I responded.

"It can only be done through fasting and prayer.", He answered. I had fasted before, but something about this fast was completely different. It began before I even left the missionary's presence.

As I was opening my car door to leave, he asked, "Can I lay hands on you and pray for you?"

"Absolutely!", I replied.

The words of his prayer have long since left my memory, but the results have remained. I began a water fast that day and for the first time in my life, all other desires were gone; removed completely. The lust that had plagued me for years was completely removed. Desire for watching sports vanished. I didn't get on Facebook or turn on the radio or television for well over 40 days. Later, during the fast, I asked the missionary about the prayer. He smiled and told me he had given me a short cut. I was truly stunned at the impact of the Spirit of God pouring into my life through this man's prayer. Out of him flowed the rivers of living water promised to each of us who believe in Jesus' name.

Apart from a bowl of oatmeal and one bowl of soup toward the beginning, the complete water fast lasted forty days. At that point, the missionary called me up, startling me with, "Mike, I've never had this happen, but God just told me you are done with your fast. The stronghold is broken!"

The next morning, I arose, and began the process of breaking the fast. A few days later the missionary came over and laid hands on Debra, praying for healing over a period of two days. Incredible things began to happen. Bones put back into place. Thinking being cleared. Convulsions being ended. My wife woke up after the second day and began cleaning the house top to bottom. She had not been able to do anything for so long! Because of this healing prayer, she was able to put together a beautiful graduation party for Daaron.

The healing was not complete, however. Debra told me, "God warned me before you even met with the missionary that it was going to be tempting, when I was healed, to quit all my treatments. But, don't do this. Keep up with the LDA, LDI, Meyers IV, and colonics." These were treatments that were not medicines, but rather immune function and nutritional boosts. My pride and arrogance were not gone, however, and reared their ugly head.

"I was the one who had done the fast!", I reasoned. "I know God has healed!" I even had the gall to tell her, "You aren't hearing God! It must be another voice!" Yet my wife had always heard God clearly and obeyed. Because of my pride, my wife suffered. God slowly chipped away, continuing to break me, melt me, and crucify me.

Since that day we have had numerous ups and downs. Debra was able to ween off the steroid she had been dependent on for over five years. That was huge, as before this time she would have inflammation which caused horrendous pain, screaming, and confusion. To this point the steroid had been the only anti-inflammatory to keep the pain, screaming, and confusion at bay. Because of my arrogance, though, we didn't continue the treatments God had told Debra to keep up with. God had to deal the death blow to the pride and arrogance still clinging to me. He did this by making me aware of some things in my life which I had long laid at the feet of Debra and her illness.

One of the issues brought to my attention was how much my attitudes shaped the culture of my home. Debra and I were always arguing. I felt I was blamed for everything and nothing I could do would change anything. Many times, the arguments were over finances or me forgetting to get something at the store, or me keeping things from Debra. Often, the arguments were simply caused by confusion in her mind due to poor liver function. During these times the stress from the prolonged illness and loss would overflow and we would begin screaming at each other. I wish I could say it only happened when Daaron wasn't at home, but that would not be true. There were times he would come roaring out of his room, screaming at Debra and swinging at me in his anger. I felt I was getting hit by both sides.

She would scream at me, "I hate this chaos! You create so much chaos in this home!"

Angrily, I would scream back, "I am NOT the cause of this chaos! YOUR stupid illness has created this chaos!"

When God corrected my thinking on this, it was like having a glass of cold water thrown over my face. I sputtered, stammered, and tried to argue. But God, in His mercy, would not allow me any way out.

Finally, I came to a point where I was at least willing to listen. God began to show me how arrogant I was thinking I could do ANYTHING apart from Him. I began to understand what it meant to take up my cross and follow Him. It meant my absolute and utter death on a daily basis. It was only as I began to die daily that my pride and arrogance began to die. As these things began to be put to death, I found peace in my home. PEACE! IN MY HOME! How could this be? The circumstances had not yet changed, not completely.

Debra's illness still demanded money be spent on treatments and tests. Though her inflammation was less, there were still many instances of confused thinking. I was still responsible for keeping track of appointments, doing dishes, cleaning the house, going to work, taking care of finances, mowing lawn, getting Daaron to school and work, etc. Exhaustion overwhelmed me. The struggle to get up early and pray was very real; more so than it had ever been.

This whole battle made me realize how everything I experienced was impossible to bear. He didn't give me more strength to get through it. Instead, he brought me to the point of death. However, at the point of death, He made me an offer. "Give up your life and accept mine." Let me repeat that here. "Give up your life and accept mine." This is very real. This, in a very real way, is the gospel. I gave up my life, completely. And, as Paul states, 'I no longer live, but Christ lives in me." And the life of Christ is more than enough to take on any challenge, any struggle, anything life in this world has to throw our way. WE ARE VICTORIOUS IN THE HANDS OF JE-SUS!!!

Chapter Eleven

Ambassadors for His Kingdom

Blessed is the God and Father of our Lord Jesus Christ, the Father of mercies and God of all comfort, who comforts us in all our troubles so that we may be able to comfort those experiencing any trouble with the comfort with which we ourselves are comforted by God.

- II Corinthians 1:3-4 NET

As I close, I realize my story is incomplete. Debra is still struggling with pain and sickness. She is inundated with negative messages which continue circling through her mind like vultures waiting to feast.

Daaron is now a twenty year old young man who has been all but crushed by the weight of this journey. He struggles in his faith. Making the decision to drop the stress of college, he works nights in a factory. And this is ok. It is where we are in our story.

However, I see something different. I am learning to press into Jesus, waiting in His presence for the breakthrough only He can bring. I know beyond a shadow of a doubt complete healing will occur. Daaron will find his footing in Christ and be used to further the kingdom. Choosing to use this exact point to finish our story, although unusual, is necessary. It is necessary because so many stories end with everything being completely resolved. But often life is not resolved. Life is a constant journey and it is my desire to encourage each of you in the midst of this journey. Don't give up. Don't quit. Walk with me, follow my family's journey as we follow Jesus. Join us as we look forward to the next chapter of life. Enter into God's world, His kingdom.

I began this book writing about leaving our world and entering into God's. In one sense this is true. In another sense, this is a total falsehood. The reality is, God invaded our world over 2000 years ago in the form of a baby boy. He entered into our difficulties, our suffering, because of a depth of love I could not possibly comprehend. This love has transformed my life moment by moment, day by day, year by year. The depth of love contained in the actions and words of our maker have overwhelmed me through our time of suffering. Because of His infinite love, He has brought us through our trials with a deeper understanding, not only of Him but of those around us, His beloved creation.

You are beloved by God. Those reading this book may have experienced very real suffering. If you are in the midst of suffering and someone handed you this book, it is my prayer that the God of all comfort flows out of the pages of this book, comforting you , encouraging you, lifting you into the mighty arms of Jesus. And please know, you are not alone. You are beloved of God.

Because of God's great love for us, He walks with us through our storms. He doesn't just go through them with us, however. He teaches us to be victorious in and through each and every storm. Sometimes these storms can seem so overwhelming we don't feel as if we will ever see the light of day. During these times it is tempting to believe we have been abandoned. These are the times we must learn to persevere in prayer, believing God hears and answers those who diligently seek Him. He does this because of His all-consuming love.

God loves us so much He will settle for nothing less than His perfect reflection shining forth from His precious metals. As we suffer, He is at work. Through His Spirit He is continually bringing us to the point of death so He can live through us. As we die, we find true, powerful life. As we live through faith in Him, we become ambassadors, representatives of His Kingdom. As ambassadors, we live with one foot in heaven and one foot on earth. And we see as Jesus sees, love as Jesus loves, live as Jesus lived. We become the perfect reflection of Jesus to a world that is hurting deeply. For this, I am grateful; grateful for being carried through the purifying fires so I can be an ambassador of His Kingdom.

As an ambassador of His Kingdom, I carry around the life of Christ in me. With His life living in me, the following things should be flowing from me to you in every word; Love, joy, peace, patience, kindness, goodness, gentleness, faithfulness, and self-control. As Paul stated, this is the fruit of the Spirit. As I die to myself, His Spirit bears fruit in me, bringing me to a life full of His fruit. Only His fruit is life giving. The Spirit alone brings forth the fruit of life through the pain of death. I am learning to embrace the pains of death daily in order to have these replaced with the fruit of the Spirit. As I do this, I become a partaker in the sufferings of Christ and am encouraged daily to do so for the joy set before me.

This joy is meant to be for all followers of Jesus. However, many will never experience this joy because they are too afraid to enter into suffering. This is seen through much of my story, as leaders of churches denied their congregants the opportunity to join us in our suffering. It is also seen in lack of persistence in prayer and fasting. As an ambassador of the kingdom of heaven, it is truly my desire to see others reach beyond their current level of "living". This can only be done as we relinquish our "rights" to ourselves, truly die to ourself daily, and take up the life, the true eternal life of Jesus the Messiah.

I close our story with it being incomplete. Yes, my wife is still struggling. My son is wrestling with life and faith. Financially we are strapped. However, I am content. I am content as I know my God answers prayer. Dying daily has brought me a strength I could never conceive of. I walk in a different world than I ever thought possible. Persevering in prayer, fasting more and more, diligently seeking God, I am convinced He loves us more deeply than we are capable of understanding. I am persuaded He will reveal himself to me, and through me, as I diligently seek Him in faith. And I know, beyond all doubt, I am an ambassador of the only Great Physician who has and will continue to heal my wife, transform my son, and use this story to comfort and revolutionize many.

God Bless you and revive your faith today!

Made in the USA
Middletown, DE
14 April 2021

37691397R00052